Maze Craze
Mummy Mazes

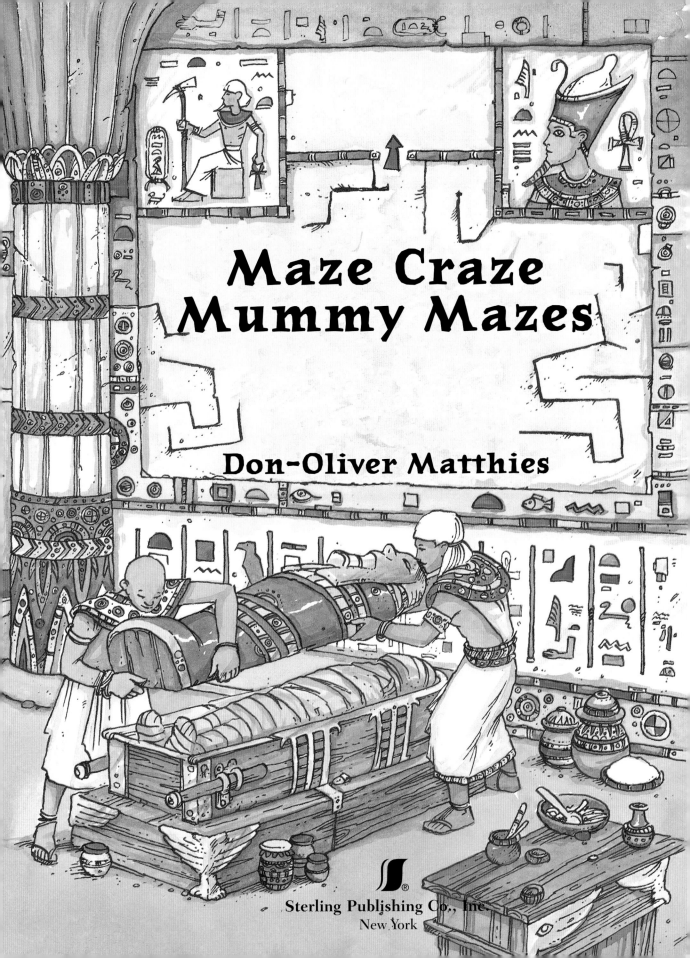

Maze Craze
Mummy Mazes

Don-Oliver Matthies

Sterling Publishing Co., Inc.
New York

Library of Congress Cataloging-in-Publication Data Available

10   9   8   7   6

Published in 2003 by Sterling Publishing Co., Inc.
387 Park Avenue South
New York, NY 10016
Originally published in Germany in 2002 under the title *Das Geheimnis
der Pyramiden* by Edition Bücherbär im Arena Verlag GmbH
Wurzburg, Germany
© 2002 by Arena Verlag GmbH
English translation © 2003 by Sterling Publishing Co., Inc.
Distributed in Canada by Sterling Publishing
c/o Canadian Manda Group, 165 Dufferin Street
Toronto, Ontario, Canada, M6K 3H6
Distributed in the United Kingdom by GMC Distribution Services,
Castle Place, 166 High Street, Lewes, East Sussex, England BN7 1XU
Distributed in Australia by Capricorn Link (Australia) Pty. Ltd.
P.O. Box 704, Windsor, NSW 2756, Australia

Sterling ISBN-13: 978-1-4027-0548-9
       ISBN-10: 1-4027-0548-4

For information about custom editions, special sales, premium and
corporate purchases, please contact Sterling Special Sales
Department at 800-805-5489 or specialsales@sterlingpub.com

Draw a picture or place a
photograph of yourself here.

This books belongs to:

Chloe

Meet Dr. Carter. He works for a
museum and specializes in solving
Egyptian mummy mazes. Are you
ready to help him on his adventure?

Dr. Carter is trying to decipher old hieroglyphics with a magnifying glass. He needs to find a couple of books on his shelf. Can you find them?

end

start

The Director of the museum tells Dr. Carter that he must travel to Egypt to research some recently discovered mummy mazes. The Director prepares him by asking if Dr. Carter can solve the maze on his wall.

The very next day, Dr. Carter sets out on his trip to Egypt. Which route does he have to take from London?

Dr. Carter finally arrives in Cairo, the capital city of Egypt. He must now find his way to the hotel. Can you help him?

In the morning, Dr. Carter walks to the bazaar. He would like to buy a carpet for his office. How can he get to the carpet dealer?

start

carpet dealer

When he arrives, Dr. Carter is quite astonished. The carpet dealer
has an authentic maze carpet for him.

On the way back to the hotel, Dr. Carter comes upon Maze Square. He must travel many paths in order to cross the Square. Where should he go?

Oasis

Dr. Carter decides to travel to the desert. He would like to excavate some ancient Egyptian artifacts. He's very thirsty though. Can you lead him to the oasis?

At the oasis, Dr. Carter meets a few camels that are tied up. Can you figure out which camel is fastened to which stake?

On the edge of the desert, Dr. Carter runs into some Bedouins, who are nomadic Arabs that live in the desert. Can you guess who lives in each tent?

Dr. Carter decides to set up camp. He puts up his tent. He would like to see his surroundings. Can you help him climb the rock to see where he is?

Dr. Carter begins to dig. The heat is getting to him and soon he only sees shovels and pickaxes everywhere. Can you find your way through the mirage?

After digging for a while, Dr. Carter finds an old roll of parchment that is a map to the Pharaoh's tomb. The eye represents the tomb. Can you find the way?

He did it! Dr. Carter found the Pharaoh's tomb. He has to enter it underground. Can you find the path to the tomb?

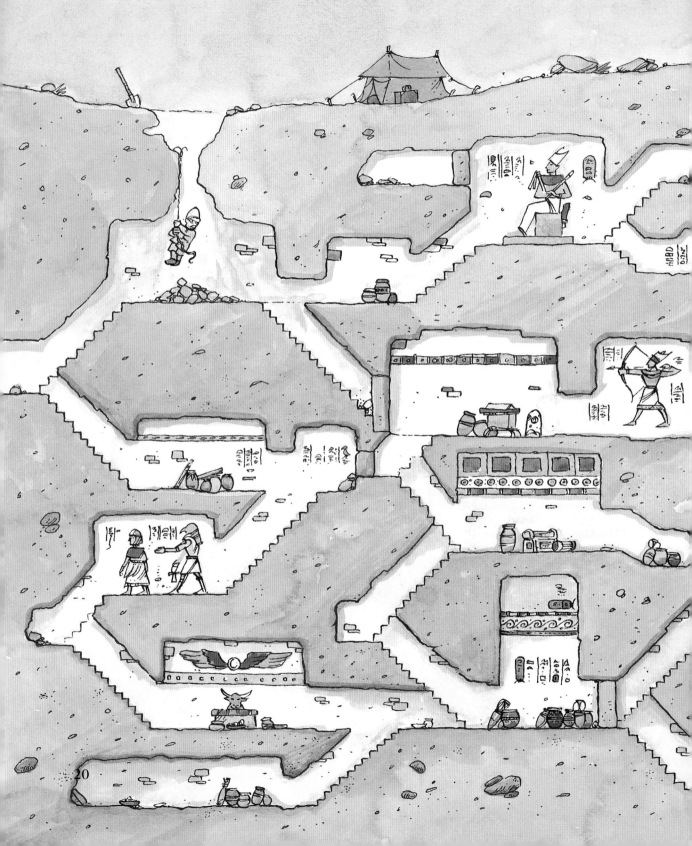

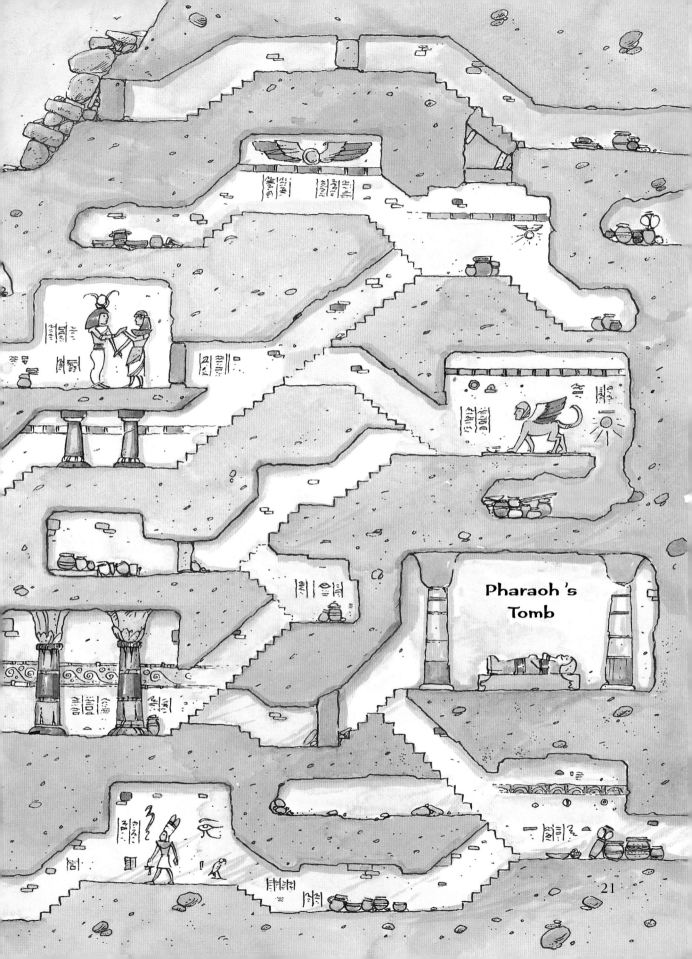

Pharaoh's Tomb

21

end

That evening, Dr. Carter reads about the Pharaohs and the Egyptians.

Dr. Carter falls asleep. He begins to dream of ancient Egypt and of mummies, just as they were described in his book. Can you solve the mazes in his dreams?

23

In ancient Egypt, the Pharaohs were buried in pyramids. In order to build a pyramid, many huge stones were needed.

The stones were then transported over the Nile, the great river in Egypt, to the pyramid's construction site.

start ▶

◀◀ end

At the construction site, the stones were stacked upon one another.
Find out which work group is heading to the ramp.

ramp

A

B

C

D

When a Pharaoh died, he was wrapped in linen bandages in order to preserve his body.

Then the Pharaoh was laid in a sarcophagus that was hidden in a special chamber inside the pyramid. Can you solve these two mazes?

The next morning Dr. Carter wakes up. He starts making breakfast. He doesn't see the small fire salamander, which is trying to grab some of his leftovers. Can you help the hungry salamander get to the food?

After breakfast, Dr. Carter repacks his things. Unfortunately, he has misplaced his glasses. Can you find the way through all the objects to his glasses?

start

Then Dr. Carter flies home. Do you see the path he has to take?

end

start

When Dr. Carter arrives home, the Director is extremely excited. "We are creating a new Egyptian maze exhibit and we would like you to be in charge!" the Director tells him. Dr. Carter couldn't be more happy!

Answers

page 6

page 7

page 8

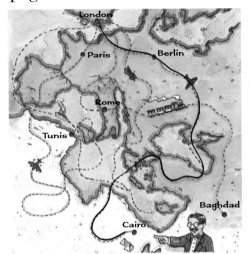

page 9

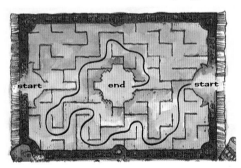

page 10

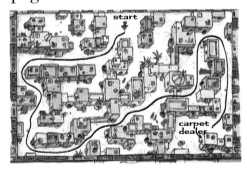

page 11

pages 12–13

page 14

page 15

1=E
2=C
3=D
4=A
5=B

page 16

1=green tent
2=black tent
3=blue tent
4=yellow tent
5=red tent

page 17

page 18

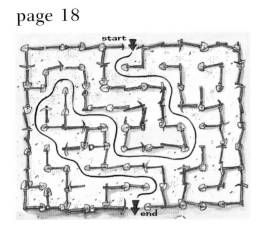

page 19

pages 20–21

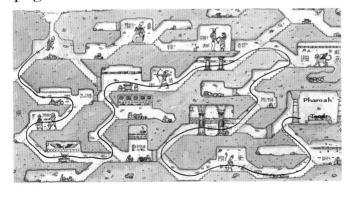

page 22

page 23

page 24

page 25

page 26

work group D

page 27

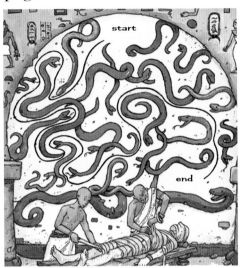

page 28

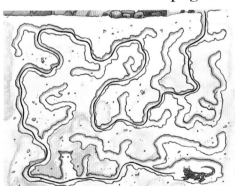

page 29

page 30

page 31

page 32

page 33